The Old
& Danson Library

Trinity College,
Oxford

The Old Library, viewed from Durham Quad.

Published by Trinity College, Oxford, 2017
Printed by Seacourt Print, Oxford
Designed by Julian Littlewood

ISBN 978-1-5272-0755-4

Front cover: The Old Library, view towards the Danson Library.
Back cover: East window 2, detail: St John the Baptist.

Contents

Acknowledgements

This guide is very much a collaborative effort, that builds on the work of previous librarians and historians, some of whom appear in the 'Further Reading' (pp. 65-66). Each section embodies contributions by people beyond those named on the contents page. Accordingly, the principal authors wish to record their gratitude to:

Stefano Evangelista (Fellow Librarian), Fiona Gameson (alumna), Clare Hopkins (Trinity Archivist), and Valerie Worth (Senior Tutor and erstwhile co-Fellow Librarian), for their expertise, their support, and their enthusiasm for the project;

The photographers who have given their time and skill with such generosity: Painton Cowan, Thomas Knollys (Trinity Alumni Relations Officer), and Juliet Ralph;

Other members of Trinity College who have contributed with their specialist knowledge, in particular Russell Dominian and Gail Trimble; Sue Broers and Kevin Knott for their support from the conception of the project; Hannah Robinson for her advice and insight; Jonathan Downing (Trinity Old Member), for text on William Blake;

Margaret Erskine and Alison Felstead, for their assistance with proofreading;

Melanie Bryant at *Country Life*; Janet Gunning from Durham Cathedral Library; Michael Stansfield and Mike Harkness from Durham University Library Archives, for their help with obtaining images and reproduction rights; Clive Taylor, Associate Lecturer at the School of Art, Design and Fashion, University of Central Lancashire, for text on metamorphic chairs;

Julian Littlewood for masterminding the layout and design, and Derek McCrae at Seacourt Printers for converting it to print.

Lastly, we would like to thank the President and Fellows of Trinity College for the value they place upon the Library and its treasures.

Foreword

The year 2017 marks the six-hundredth anniversary of Trinity College's Old Library. While the College itself was founded only in 1555, its first members moved into a quadrangle that was already more than a century old, having previously belonged to the Benedictine Abbey of St Cuthbert in Durham. Trinity's founder, Sir Thomas Pope (*c.* 1507–1559), initially intended the College to be a training house for Catholic priests. Pope took an interest in the Library and sent a large consignment of books and manuscripts that he had acquired to stock the empty shelves. Ever since, the Library has been a vital resource. Nowadays the College's main library, inaugurated in 1928, is the working hub of its graduate and undergraduate communities, while the Old Library and the Danson Library are home to its historical collections, which, as readers will discover, include many rare and precious items. This guide (a revision of its predecessor produced in 1988) brings together the expertise of Sharon Cure, the current Librarian, with that of Alan Coates (Old Member and Honorary Librarian of the Old Library), and Richard Gameson (Old Member and Professor of the History of the Book, Durham University). It provides a comprehensive introduction to the history and some of the highlights of Trinity's collections, as well as to the spectacular medieval glass and special furniture housed in the Old Library.

Trinity's libraries have always been at the heart of the College, providing a repository of knowledge and a working space for its students and Fellows – a particularly captivating one in the case of the Old Library. The collections have grown steadily over the years, thanks to the work of generations of librarians and generous donations. At the same time, rare and historical material is continuously the object of preservation work, which aims to ensure that it is handed down to future generations in the best possible state. We hope that readers will enjoy this tour of our historical buildings and collections.

Stefano Evangelista, Fellow in English and Fellow Librarian
March 2017

Sketch of the Old Library by W. H. Pyne
(Trinity College Archives)

The Old Library

Durham College Library

In 1290 the monks of Durham Cathedral Priory erected their college in Oxford on a site which they had owned since 1286, lying to the north of Broad Street. The early years of its existence should be seen against a background of financial instability. This was alleviated, at least partially, by the re-founding of the College by Thomas Hatfield, Bishop of Durham. On 1 March 1381, shortly before his death, he covenanted £3,000 to provide an annual income of 200 marks for the foundation. The College was dedicated to the 'most holy Trinity, the most blessed Virgin and the most glorious confessor Cuthbert', and special prayers were to be said for Hatfield and his family, and for Edward III and Queen Philippa. The College was still a cell of the Priory, but with a greater degree of independence than it had previously enjoyed. However, it was not until the beginning of the fifteenth century that the financial position of the College became stable enough to allow large-scale building including a new chapel and library. The monastic College was finally dissolved in 1539, along with Durham Priory. The buildings and land were eventually purchased by an Oxfordshire landowner and courtier, Sir Thomas Pope, who founded Trinity College on the site.

In 1336 Pope Benedict XII issued constitutions on higher study by monks, including the stipulation that one in twenty monks should attend one of the universities. Of the many Durham monks who received a university education at the Oxford College during the later Middle Ages, few remained more than six years; indeed, for the majority, the College seems to have been little more than a finishing school, before they returned north to take up administrative positions in the hierarchy of the mother house or one of its other cells. One or two monks did establish themselves permanently in the College, although fewer examples of this are to be found at Durham College than at Canterbury College, the Oxford foundation of another Benedictine cathedral priory. To facilitate the monks' studies, Pope Benedict required abbots and priors of monasteries to choose books to be made available to the students.

Clearly a library was needed. The first reference to a library building at Durham College does not occur until 1417, when an entry in the College account book (below) records the building of the library, with specially purchased timber, at a cost of £42; contributions towards the cost of the building came from Durham Priory and from other Durham cells.

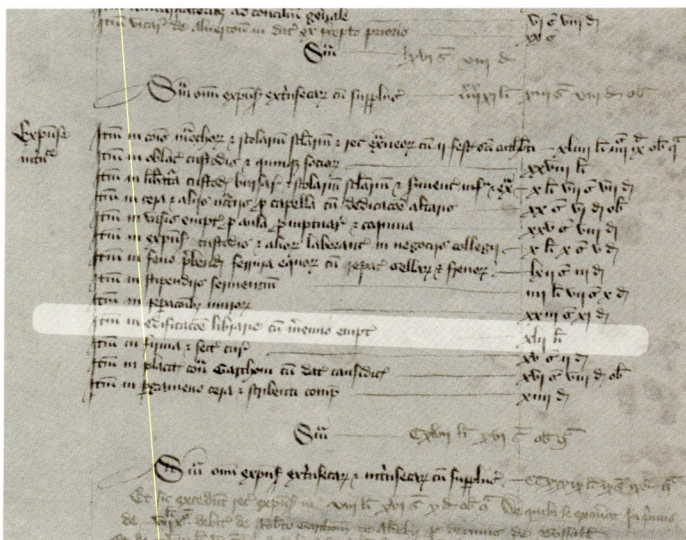

In the year 1417, a total of £147 16s and three farthings was accounted for as 'Expensae intrinsece' (internal expenses). Of this, the considerable sum of £42 (lxij li) was spent 'in edificatione librarie cum meremio empto' (in building a library with purchased timber).

This must have placed some burden on the mother house's finances, for the Priory was, at the same time, building a library of its own. However, the Priory clearly had support from Bishop Thomas Langley (1406–1437), who is known to have contributed £10 towards the construction of the library and chambers in the College. Most of the work in Oxford seems to have been completed by 1418, and much of the exterior stonework remains to this day, as part of Trinity's Old Library. The dimensions of the Library were 27 by 18 feet, only about half as long as its counterpart in Durham. The stonework of the south window is interesting, in that it is an example of a style transitional between

Early English and Decorated. Although the present, seventeenth-century ceiling is flat, the fact that it comes down below the level of the top of the south window shows that the original medieval ceiling was barrel-shaped.

The Library was not finally fitted out for use until 1431–32, when the accounts record a payment of £6 16s 8d for it to be furnished with lecterns and 'other necessary items'. It is not known exactly what form this furnishing took, but it may be assumed that it consisted of two-sided lecterns, probably running out from the windows. This was the arrangement of the library rooms at All Souls College and New College. Various payments are also recorded from the last quarter of the fourteenth century to the last quarter of the fifteenth century for binding and chaining of books in the Library.

By the mid-fourteenth century, most secular Oxford colleges had two collections of books: the chained collection, from which no borrowing was allowed; and, for loan, a collection of books which circulated among the Fellows. However, although Durham College had its reference collection, it is not clear that it also had a circulating library.

Front view of the Old Library.

The arrangements for the use of the reference collection would probably have been similar to those in operation at All Souls, where each Fellow had a key to the library, although nothing could be borrowed from it. It must be assumed that Durham College had a librarian, since someone would have had responsibility for taking new books into the collection and for chaining, but, as at All Souls, there is no record of the identity of this figure. In both cases it was, perhaps, the Sub-Warden (the deputy head of the College).

The main source for Durham College's books was Durham Cathedral Priory, chiefly its 'Spendement' collection – the Priory's book store – but also the main cloister library. Nevertheless, several donations are recorded by members of the community. Unfortunately, the bequest of Bishop Richard de Bury of Durham's books, presumably destined for Durham College, was not honoured, because Richard died in debt in 1345 and his extensive library had to be sold.

Four lists of books sent to Oxford from Durham survive from the period before the second decade of the fifteenth century. Most of these books were theological texts, biblical commentaries, or works of the Church Fathers; there is very little canon or civil law, hardly any history, and no classical texts. A catalogue of books at Durham College, dating from the last decade of the fourteenth century, reveals a more complete picture of the books in use: in addition to the commentaries on biblical texts, patristics, and other theological treatises, there are two sections of philosophy and logic, numbering some thirty-seven volumes. There are also three medical texts and a miscellaneous collection, which includes a life of St Cuthbert, more theology, and two canon law books. In general, the Benedictines at Oxford graduated in canon law as well as in theology. However, the Durham monks were the exception to this, only taking degrees in theology.

Fresh consignments of books were sent from Durham to Oxford in 1418, 1419, and 1434–35. Numbers which were written at the head of the fore-edge of several of these books, now in Durham Cathedral Library, may refer to the shelves on which they were kept in the library at Durham College. Some surviving volumes also bear the inscription 'deram college'.

What happened to the contents of Durham College's library at the Dissolution of the Monasteries? One can only speculate about the fate of the furnishings: they may still have been in position when Pope acquired the

Rear view of the Old Library and of the Danson Library, from the lawns.

property, and then have been removed in the refit of 1625 (see below); or the woodwork may have been pilfered or sold during the late 1540s, as happened later at the dispersal of Duke Humfrey's University Library. Those volumes inscribed 'deram college' found their way back to Durham. Certain books and manuscripts seem to have been obtained by individuals, including Thomas Allen, Fellow of Trinity, and thence to have passed into the hands of collectors, such as Kenelm Digby, William Laud, and Robert Harley, and from them to the Bodleian Library and the British Museum (later British Library).

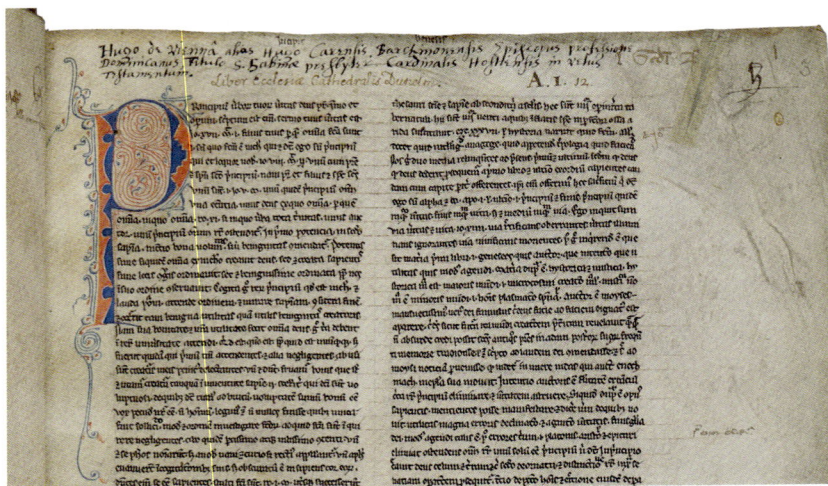

Durham Cathedral Library, MS A.1.12, a mid-thirteenth-century copy of Hugh of Saint-Cher's commentaries on Old Testament books from Genesis to Esther.

This is probably the best-documented manuscript associated with Durham College, demonstrably there in 1417. A contemporary note records that it had been given to Durham Cathedral Priory by Bertram of Middleton, monk then Prior (1244-58) of the community. As the inscription styles him Prior, the donation was presumably made while he held that office. A Priory library catalogue of 1392 reveals that the volume had been consigned to the Spendement. In 1409 it was one of fourteen volumes dispatched to Durham College, as recorded on a list of 'the books sent on a second occasion to Oxford by John Washington the chancellor, with the considered mandate of the prior and convent of Durham [...] 14 October 1409'. An audit of the Spendement collection on 5 October 1416 confirmed that it was still in Oxford seven years later: the entry in the relevant Durham library catalogue was not dotted (as were those for all the books found to be present and correct), and it had 'Oxon' written beside it.

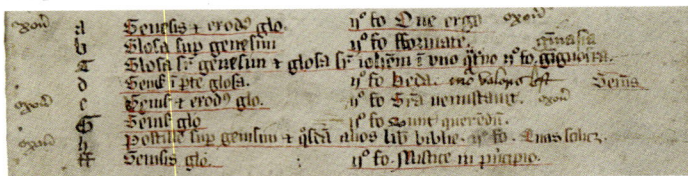

A letter of 1436 by Prior Washington responding to the Archbishop of York's expressed interest in these commentaries, noted that the 'better-written copy [...] is held in our college in Oxford', and undertook to withdraw it in order to have a copy made for the Archbishop. The manuscript presumably returned to Durham shortly thereafter.

The Old Library, Trinity College

After the Dissolution of the Monasteries, the site and buildings of Durham College passed through various hands, until, in 1555, they were sold to Sir Thomas Pope, who received letters patent in March of that year from the crown (Philip and Mary), establishing the College of the Holy and Undivided Trinity. The same dedication had also formed one element of the tripartite dedication of Durham College. The first President, Thomas Slythurst, and the new Fellows, mostly from The Queen's or Exeter Colleges, were admitted on Lady Day 1556. Thomas Pope's interest in the College continued until his death in 1559, when his wife, Elizabeth, took his place as patron.

The Old Library was and still is the Fellows' Library. Undergraduates have sometimes received special permission to use it – John Henry Newman, for example, during the vacations of 1819–20 – but the books for their use, when such collections existed, were housed elsewhere.

The exterior features of the Old Library are broadly the same as they were in the days of Durham College, with two notable exceptions. First, the dormer

The Old Library, view towards the south window.

7

rooms above the Library were added in 1602, by President Kettell; secondly, the windows on the western (Durham Quad) side of the Library underwent extensive alterations in the eighteenth century.

Although the exterior of the Library retains many similarities to the period of its use by Durham College, the same is not true of the interior. The ceiling was lowered slightly, and flattened, to accommodate the dormer rooms added by Kettell. A survey made in 1541 noted that the Library was well supplied with desks and had a sound floor and ceiling. However, the furniture seems to have been removed, certainly by the second decade of the seventeenth century. Edward Hyndmer, a Fellow of Trinity in 1568, at his death in 1618 left his books and a sum of money to the College to allow the Library to be refitted to accommodate the new books, a process which began in 1625. The extent of his gift was revealed in 1890, when the College President, Dr Blakiston, discovered on almost all the present bookcases, under a thick coating of paint, the inscription 'Edwardi Hyndmeri donum' (the gift of Edward Hyndmer). Unfortunately, all of these inscriptions were removed when the paint was stripped away, except for one now slightly retouched example, which lacks the word 'donum'. At some stage between 1541 and c. 1850, the length of the Library was apparently extended, the original entrance probably having been through a partition wall where bookcases of sections T and B now stand. The area now enclosed by the bookcases of sections A, B, T, U, and V appears to have been a landing, accommodating overflow from the main library. Major structural work was required in 1986: steel supports were inserted below false floors in each bay, and wooden beams were added within the cases in order to make the whole building structurally sound.

From the beginning, the books in the Old Library were chained, effectively as a reference collection. The College's Statutes made provision for a circulating library as well, and it was long considered doubtful that one ever existed. However, a note recently discovered in Hyndmer's notebook gives a list of books and records that they were distributed among the Fellows and Scholars. This seems to be the only mention in the College's records of that period for the loan of books, so it remains uncertain whether it happened regularly or whether this was an isolated instance.

The furniture in the Old Library, after the Hyndmer refit, resembled that of other contemporary libraries, including the cases now in Duke Humfrey's

Library in the Bodleian. Although the desks have been removed at Trinity, some of the cases still show scars, and there is also evidence on some cases of the holes used for the chaining rods which ran under the desks. Trinity chained its books from the foundation until the middle of the eighteenth century. This was an expensive item in a college's finances, so that when benefactors, such as Pope, sent chains with their gifts or bequests, they were deemed worthy of special thanks. There are frequent references in the Library accounts during the eighteenth century to chaining and unchaining. An especially large bill of £6 3s 8d paid to a smith in 1765 may mark the removal of most of the chains; however, a smith was still being paid for work, presumably to do with chains, in 1779. Trinity's policy with regard to chaining seems anachronistic: most other Oxford libraries had ceased to chain their books by *c.* 1700, and the process had been abandoned in Cambridge nearly a century earlier, with the increasing cheapness and availability of books in small formats.

It is not known when the desks were removed from the bookcases. However, the cases themselves were altered after 1850: they were raised to the ceiling in order to house the library of President James Ingram, who had died in 1850,

Eighteenth-century Library catalogue with chain remnant.

and left his books to the College. This bequest doubled the size of the Library. A glance at the edges of the cases reveals the extent of the alterations. It is possible that, at this time, the number of extra cases placed on the landing to house overflow had to be increased to such an extent that it seemed more appropriate to incorporate the landing into the library proper by removing the partition wall and extending the Library to its present length of 36 feet.

Although the College had a library from its foundation, there is no record of there having been a librarian before 1629–30, when an entry in the College accounts notes that he was paid five shillings per term. Magdalen had appointed a Mr Bull to be Librarian in 1550: he was the first salaried Fellow Librarian of a college in Oxford; he, too, was paid five shillings per term. Trinity continued to pay its Librarian at this rate until 1651, when the stipend was increased to £1 per year; from 1661, this was paid out of the Hartfield Bequest (see below). Unfortunately, the names of the Librarians are not recorded. In 1726 the Library was given its own accounts, which note the income and expenditure, but, again, do not name the Librarian, until 1767–68, when Thomas Warton was listed as Vice-President and Librarian. It is, therefore, possible that the Vice-President had been responsible for the Library from the foundation. The link persisted until the middle of the nineteenth century; the two posts seem then to have been separated.

There is no mention of the Librarian in the early Statutes of the College, although one chapter is devoted to the running of the Library. The regulations are essentially conservative, and contain a number of features which were standard to Oxford college libraries. For example, all books given to the Library had to be marked clearly with the names of the College and of the donor. The Statutes further laid down strict rules about who was to use the Library – it was only to be open to the President and graduates of the College. Anyone who broke the rules was to be fined.

Today the Old Library is still used by the Fellows of the College for their own work and teaching. However, the books are also consulted more frequently than in the past both by Trinity's own students for dissertations and seminars, and by students and academics from all over the world for their studies. It is also opened regularly for College events and for special visits by interested groups and individuals; it has been a location for several films and television series, including *Testament of Youth* and *Endeavour*.

The Old Library in 1930
(Country Life, *1 March 1930, p. 322*).

Notable Books

At the time when Trinity was founded, the traditional method of acquiring books for college libraries was by donation, both from outsiders and, more often, from bequests from Fellows, when they either took up clerical livings or died. Trinity seems to have followed this procedure, at least for the first fifty years of its existence: indeed, it bought hardly any new books until the presidency of Ralph Kettell, by the end of which it was able to use money from the Hartfield Bequest. The books bought at this stage were mostly classics, although there was also some theology. By the end of the sixteenth century, other colleges, including Corpus Christi and University College, were using donations of money for library purchases. Thereafter, Trinity acquired new books by purchase and donation. Donations were recorded in the benefactors' books in addition to being recorded as such in the books themselves.

The first and largest of the early gifts to the Library came from the Founder, Sir Thomas Pope: he appears to have given ninety-one volumes, including twenty-six manuscripts. Twenty-seven of the printed books bear

the cancelled inscription 'ex grenewych' and fifteen 'ex hampton court'. These were probably acquired by Pope during the reign of Edward VI, when some of the contents of the Royal Libraries at Greenwich Palace and at Hampton Court were being disposed of as duplicates. Pope's bequest was mainly theological in content.

The books bequeathed by Pope have been preserved almost intact in the College; this may have been due to respect for the memory of the College's Founder. Books left by other early benefactors did not fare quite as well. Thomas Rawe, Canon of Windsor, left thirty-nine books to the College in 1557, but only eighteen now survive. At least seven had to be destroyed in 1808: they and other volumes had been found the previous year, walled up in the vestry, under the south end of the Library, and were in such a bad state that they could only be disposed of, their title-pages alone being retained and mounted in a scrapbook. The same fate befell a number of books left by Thomas Allen (1540–1632) and Thomas Slythurst (c. 1507/09–1560?). Other large, early bequests included those of President Ralph Kettell (1563–1643) and Francis Combes (*fl.* 1601–41).

However, the most influential bequest to the Library between Pope's and that of James Ingram was, undoubtedly, that of Richard Rands. Rands had been a Fellow of the College before his appointment to the Rectory of Hartfield; he died in 1640, leaving land to the College in his will to provide £20 annually for the College Library. This bequest formed the basis of the Library's income from 1640 until the middle of the nineteenth century, with graduation fees for the BA degrees, and fines, being added later. The so-called 'Hartfield Bequest' was to allow the College to purchase books in greater quantity than had hitherto been possible.

James Ingram's bequest of his books led, as noted, to the raising of the bookcases in the Library. Ingram was a polymath and his personal library was as varied as it was large. Not only did he possess many volumes on travel and topography, but also much historical and linguistic material, particularly in Anglo-Saxon (of which he had been Professor), French, German, and Dutch, and a number of works in the Scandinavian languages. There were also quantities of scientific books, classics, theological tracts, and miscellaneous scrapbooks of cuttings, jottings, drawings, and articles, almost all of these being heavily annotated in Ingram's distinctively scrawling hand.

Although Trinity was the first college in Oxford to attempt to provide books for its undergraduates, with a library room under the Old Library instituted in 1683, it was not until the 1920s that a purpose-built student library was planned. The War Memorial Library, built by subscription to commemorate College members killed in the First World War, was completed in 1928. That Library was initially stocked with donated books and also with post-1800 books moved from the Old Library.

The Old Library still possesses a number of library catalogues, the first dating from about 1728; there is a separate list of books (presumably the more important ones and the manuscripts) kept in a chest, from about 1697. The most recent of these catalogues consists of two large folio volumes, arranged alphabetically by author. There is also a shelf-list which complements it; both seem to date from fairly soon after Ingram's bequest, c. 1850–60, and so provide an interesting picture of what the Library was like in the middle of the nineteenth century. Virtually all of the books in the Old Library have been added to SOLO, Oxford University's on-line catalogue, and the detailed records can be viewed via the internet. Borrowers' registers exist for the Library, the present one having been in use since 1859.

The Old Library, as it is today, represents a typical example of a working college library of the eighteenth and early nineteenth centuries. It numbers some 6,000 volumes and its main strength lies in classics, theology, and county history, but it is also well supplied with biography, geography, general history, and reference books, and it contains a small but interesting collection of scientific and medical material.

Some notable books from the Old Library are described and illustrated on the following pages.

The Old Library, west window 2.

Alexander of Hales, *Expositio super tres libros Aristotelis de anima*

(Oxford: Theodoric Rood, 1481)

This commentary on Aristotle's *On the Soul* was a standard university textbook in the Middle Ages. The identity of the author has been the subject of much academic discussion but is now thought to have been Alexander de Bonino, a Franciscan who eventually became Minister General of the Order, and died in 1314.

Little is known for certain about the printer, Dietrich Rode or Theodoric Rood, except that he came to Oxford from Cologne in 1480, and was working here from 1481 until probably the middle 1480s. His workshop was in a house on the High Street. He may have been the man identified as Theodoricus Molner, stepson of the Cologne printer, Arnold ter Hoernen; there is a resemblance between the types used by both men. The book is one of the first to be printed in Oxford, and the first where the printer is identified by name.

The Trinity copy, of which the decorated initial page is displayed, belonged to Francis Combes, a Trinity man and distant relative of Sir Thomas Pope, who left a large number of books to the College in 1641.

Ptolemy, *Geographia,* trans. Jacobus Angelus

(Strasbourg: Johann Schott, 1520)

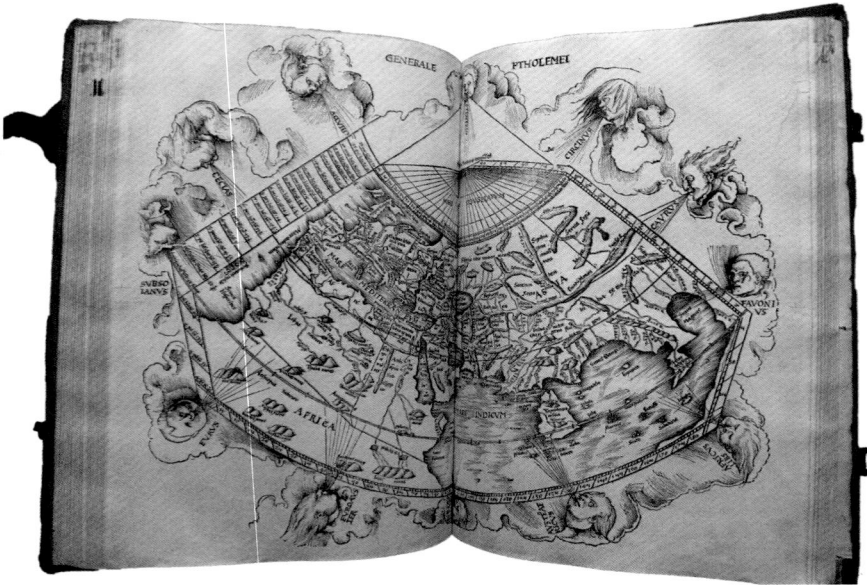

Claudius Ptolemaeus was born *c.* AD 90 in Egypt and was known as a mathematician, geographer, astronomer, and astrologer. He lived in Egypt under Roman rule, but few reliable details of his life are known. He died in Alexandria around AD 168.

Ptolemy was the author of several scientific treatises some of which were of continuing importance to later Islamic and European science. These include the *Geographia*, which is a thorough discussion of the geographic knowledge of the Greco-Roman world. The *Geographia* relies somewhat on the work of an earlier geographer, Marinos of Tyre, and on gazetteers of the Roman and ancient Persian Empires. Ptolemy was aware that he knew about only a quarter of the globe, and an erroneous extension of China southward suggests his sources did not reach all the way to the Pacific Ocean. The maps in surviving manuscripts of Ptolemy's *Geographia* date from only about 1300, after the text was rediscovered by Maximus Planudes.

Trinity's copy of the *Geographia* is bound in a sixteenth-century Oxford roll binding, with gold-tooled labels to the spine. It was given to the College by the Founder, Sir Thomas Pope, and bears his signature.

Anton Broickwy, *In quattuor Evangelia enarrationes*
(Cologne: Peter Quentel, 1539)

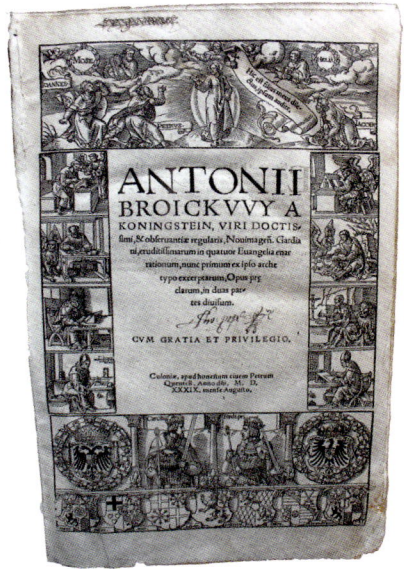

Broickwy, (*c.* 1470–1541), the author of this set of commentaries on the Gospels, was a German Franciscan and preacher. Trinity's copy formerly belonged to Henry VIII's library at Greenwich Palace. It had probably been supplied to Henry VIII by Thomas Berthelet (*c.* 1490–1555), the King's Printer, around 1545. It is bound in white buckskin, and likely to be the work of the so-called 'Greenwich Binder'. The characteristic features of this binder's works are that his royal shield is made up of small tools, and the edges of the leaves of books bound by him bear the following inscription, in gilt: 'Rex in aeternum vive' (May the King live for ever).

The Royal Librarian, Bartholomew Traheron, probably withdrew the volume from the library, with a number of others, in 1549. It was acquired by Sir Thomas Pope, who inscribed his elaborate autograph on the title page, and may have cancelled the 'ex grenewych' inscription. This was one of forty-two books from the royal libraries which Pope gave to Trinity in 1555.

Conrad Gesner, *Historiæ animalium*
lib. I, *De quadrupedibus viviparis*

(Zurich: Christoph Froschauer, 1551)

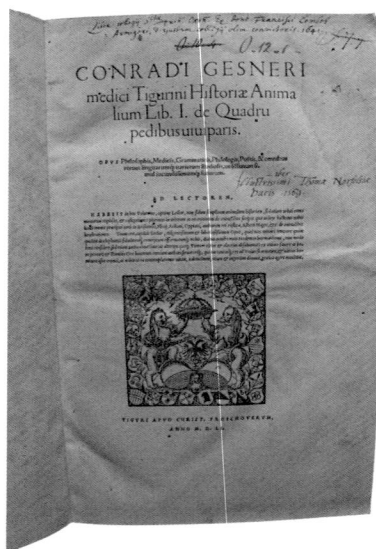

Conrad Gesner, born 1516, was a Swiss naturalist and bibliographer. After taking the degree of doctor of medicine at Basel he obtained the post of Lecturer in Physics at the Carolinum, the precursor of the University of Zurich. He died of the plague in 1565.

Gesner had a startling range of interests, reflected in his writings. These include a Greek dictionary; a catalogue of all authors who had ever written in Latin, Greek, or Hebrew; an account of approximately 130 different languages; and many works of botany.

His magnum opus was the *Historiæ animalium* (Accounts of animals), published at Zurich, 1551–58, a 4500-page encyclopaedia of animals, now regarded as the starting point of modern zoology. In it, Gesner attempted to list and describe all of the world's animals. The account includes the place of each animal within literary tradition. The pages illustrated here include a rhinoceros, based on Dürer's 1513 woodcut; the legendary sea monster, Ziphius (both opposite); and a satyr (above).

The Old Library's copy of *Historiae animalium* is bound in sixteenth-century London calf over wooden boards. It originally belonged to Thomas Howard, Duke of Norfolk (1538–1572) who made his own annotations throughout. It was bequeathed to the College by Francis Combes.

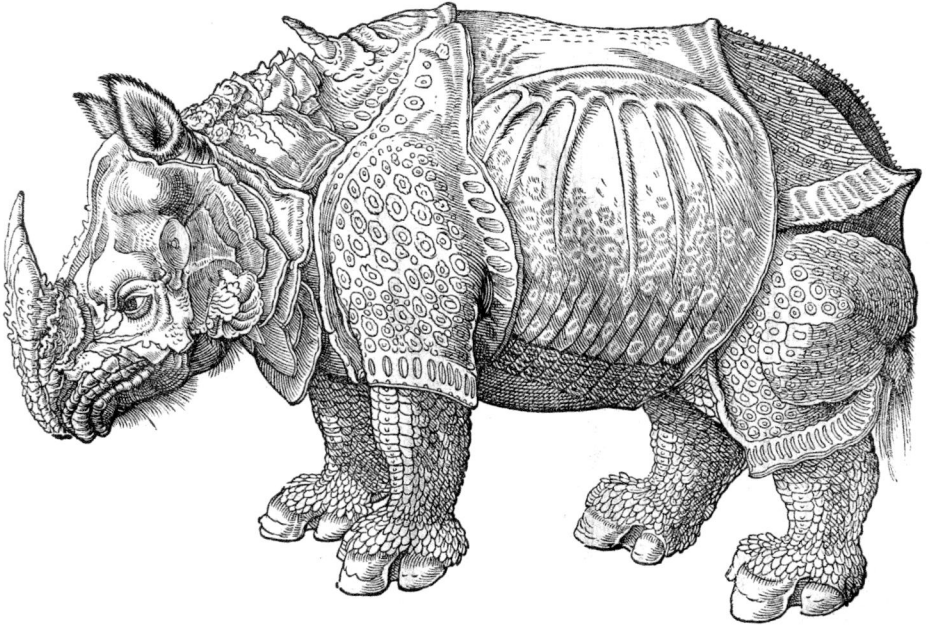

John Gerard, *The Herball,* enlarged & emended by Thomas Johnson

(London: Adam Islip et al., 1633)

The period from 1530 to 1640 was a golden age for the production of herbals as Renaissance botanists worked to revise and correct the works of earlier writers and to include the discovery of previously unknown plants brought over from the Americas. It was expected that plant locations would be included in these new herbals; Gerard's 1597 publication of *The Herball* served as the exemplum.

John Gerard (1545–1612) was a barber-surgeon, herbalist and superintendent of Lord Burghley's gardens. The production of *The Herball* was initiated by printer John Norton who had commissioned a new translation of Dodoen's 1569 *Herbal* which he planned to accompany with new and improved illustrations. After the first commissioned author died, leaving the volume unfinished, Norton hired Gerard to finish the work.

The second edition of *The Herball*, published 1633, was edited by Thomas Johnson, an apothecary and botanist who lived in London, under commission from the heirs to Gerard's estate. His edition contained many corrections and new information based on empirical observation, along with a large number of new illustrations, which are hand-coloured in the Trinity copy.

Trinity's copy was given to the College by Dr Henry Glemham, who matriculated at Trinity in 1618. He was later Dean of Bristol (1660) and Bishop of St Asaph (1667–70).

4 *Tulipa Coccinea serotina.*
Late flouring Tulipa.

Gerhard Johann Vossius, *De historicis graecis*

(Lyon: John Maire, 1624)

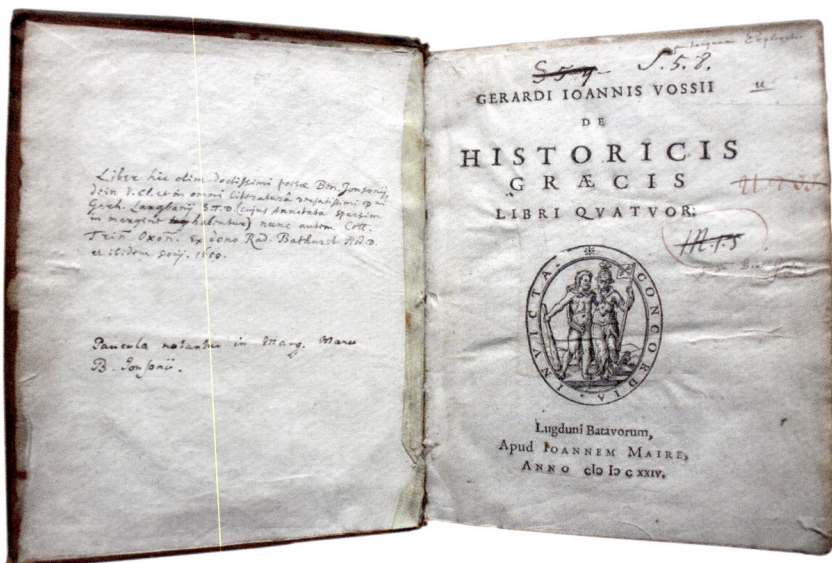

De historicis graecis (On the Greek historians) was one of the principal works of the Dutch classical scholar and theologian Gerhard Johann Vossius (1577–1649). Vossius was Regent of the theological college at Leiden University from 1615 to 1619 but, after coming under suspicion for heresy, had to resign his post, and in 1631 left Leiden for Amsterdam, where he became Professor of History. In the meantime, he had also been installed, through the influence of Archbishop William Laud, as prebend of Canterbury.

There are two inscriptions of ownership in this volume: one records that the book belonged to Ben Jonson (1572–1637), the poet and playwright, and bears his marginalia; the other, that it was owned by Jonson and Dr Gerard Langbaine (1608/09–1658), the Oxford scholar and Provost of The Queen's College, and has the latter's annotations. There are, in fact, two sets of marginal notes, in different hands: one seems to have been Jonson's, the other is probably Langbaine's. The book was subsequently acquired by Dr Ralph Bathurst (President of Trinity from 1664 to his death in 1704). He presented it to the College in 1659.

Robert Hooke, *Micrographia*

(London: John Martyn & James Allestry, 1665)

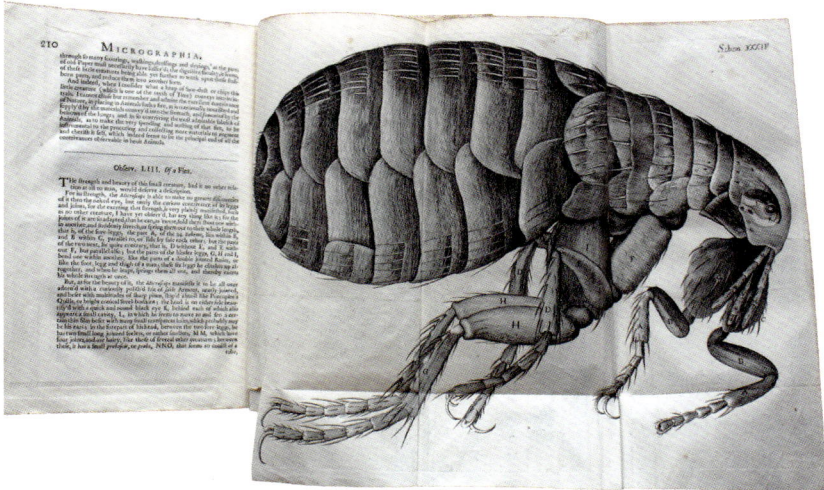

Robert Hooke was born on the Isle of Wight in 1635. He came to Oxford in 1653 to join some of the most reputable scientists of the day, in time becoming an assistant to the chemist Robert Boyle. Hooke became Curator of Experiments for the recently formed Royal Society of London in 1662. A prolific inventor, he designed a compound microscope and illumination system which he used in demonstrations at meetings. The *Micrographia* is a record of Hooke's observations using this new microscope. Hooke's work was remarkable for the accuracy and completeness of his descriptions, and the book became a bestseller in his lifetime.

Although hampered by difficult relations with contemporary luminaries such as Sir Isaac Newton, Hooke still left his mark on science. He formulated Hooke's Law, which describes the linear variation of tension with extension in an elastic spring. He also coined the term 'cells' to describe the most basic elements of cork tissue as he saw them under the microscope. The divisions in the tissue are said to have reminded him of the cells of a monastery. After the Great Fire destroyed much of London in 1666, Hooke became a surveyor and worked with Wren to redesign many of London's streets and buildings. He died in 1703.

This copy of *Micrographia* was bequeathed to Trinity by Hooke's fellow Royal Society founder, Ralph Bathurst.

David Loggan, *Oxonia Illustrata*

(Oxford: Clarendon Press, 1675)

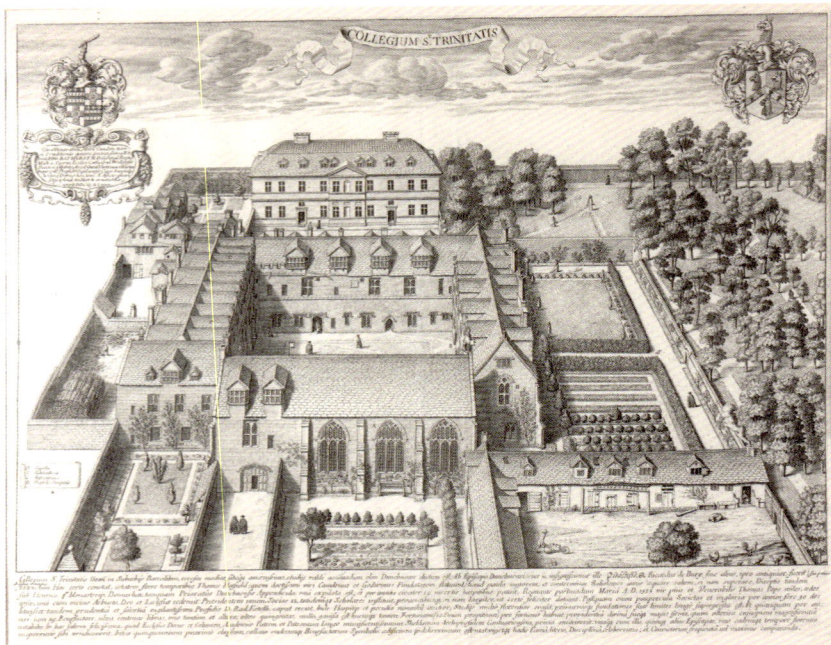

The engraving shown is the work of David Loggan (1635–c. 1700), a Pole from Danzig, who had arrived in England by the year 1653, and came to live at Nuffield, near Oxford. In 1669 he was appointed Engraver to the University of Oxford, and became a naturalised Englishman in 1675, after his marriage. *Oxonia Illustrata*, printed in Oxford in 1675, consists of some forty plates: these illustrations include view of colleges and also of other University buildings, such as the Bodleian Library, and, in addition, a plan of the city of Oxford.

The plate of Trinity shows how the College looked in 1675: at that time, the main entrance to the College was located through the door next to the Chapel. Note the medieval chapel (erected 1406–08) of the former Durham College, and, on the opposite side of the Durham Quadrangle, the old residential accommodation of Durham College. The south window of the Old Library is also clearly visible.

William Williams, *Oxonia Depicta*

(Oxford: William Williams, [1733])

This view of the College is contained in *Oxonia Depicta*, the series of engravings made by the draughtsman, William Williams, in 1732–33, and which were perhaps intended to serve as a latter-day version of David Loggan's *Oxonia Illustrata*.

The new chapel (built in the 1690s) has taken the place of Durham College's chapel, although the Old Library is unchanged. The biggest change since Loggan is visible in the gardens. In layout, they clearly represent the formality of the seventeenth century. The lime avenue was planted in 1713, but has, in the engraving, been doubled in width by Williams. Some limes, probably not original, still grow here. On the left-hand side of the engraving is the maze or labyrinth, described in a contemporary guide to Oxford as being one 'in which 'tis easy for a man to lose himself'. The author and poet Robert Southey (1774–1843) records that the maze was still in existence in 1813.

The Danson Library
and Collection

The books in the Danson bequest to Trinity College represent the collecting interests of three generations of the Danson family. The collection was begun by John Towne Danson (1817–98). He was born in Stratford-Upon-Avon, the son of William Danson, a solicitor, who had married the daughter of Charles Towne, the animal and landscape painter. J. T. Danson, like his father, entered the legal profession, becoming a barrister at the Middle Temple. He was also active on the London intellectual scene, both as a writer on economic and political affairs, and as a journalist, and was engaged by Charles Dickens, then the editor, to write leaders for the Daily News in 1845. Around 1850, because of ill-health, he retired to the country, married and then took up farming. At some point before 1860, he moved to Liverpool, and became secretary, then head of the newly-founded Thames and Mersey Marine Insurance Company, subsequently to become part of the Royal Liverpool Insurance Group. He was heavily involved in promoting education in the north west of England, and in the establishment of Liverpool University. He was also interested in antiquities, especially Roman, and those from the potteries in the Nene Valley near Northampton. It seems likely that J. T. Danson saw the books in his library as a working collection, using it to support his various intellectual activities, although he was also clearly a bibliophile who collected volumes of interest.

When he died in 1898, his son, Francis Chatillon Danson (1855–1926) inherited the family property, including his father's library. Sir Francis (knighted in 1920) was, like his father, actively engaged in the promotion of education, sitting on the councils or boards of numerous societies and institutions, including Liverpool University; he was also closely involved in industry in Liverpool, particularly shipping, and founded the firm of F. C. Danson and Company, Average Adjusters, with offices in both Liverpool and London. However, his interests were broad, and he was both a Fellow of the Society of Antiquaries of London, and a member of the Liverpool Institute of Archaeology; his entry in *Who's Who* records his recreations as 'motoring, collecting books and antiquities'. Francis Danson was also responsible for forming the family's archaeological collections. These included Egyptian antiquities, Roman glass, Greek and Etruscan pottery, and British stone and bronze axes, and were bequeathed to the Merseyside County Museums (now National Museums and Galleries on Merseyside) by his son, for display in Liverpool Museum.

Francis's eldest son, Francis Rudolf Danson, who matriculated at Trinity in 1910, was killed in action at Gallipoli in 1915. So, on the death of Sir Francis in 1926, his younger son, John Raymond ('Ray') Danson (1893–1976), took over the family home in Birkenhead, and the country house, Dry Close, in Grasmere in the Lake District. This had been built by his grandfather, J. T. Danson, in 1882, and all three generations of the family in turn retired to it. Ray attended Sedbergh School, of which his father was a governor, and followed his brother to Trinity, matriculating in 1912, to read Law. During the First World War, Ray Danson served in the Cheshire Regiment, at Gallipoli (1915), in Egypt and Palestine (1915–18), and in France (1918–19).

Library at Dry Close, Grasmere.

He was awarded the Military Cross in January 1919. After the War, he joined the family firm of average adjusters in Liverpool. His main collecting activity was devoted to the library, although there is also some indication that he was interested in philately, anecdotal evidence suggests that he did not share his father's passion for archaeology.

Ray Danson had first approached his old college with regard to leaving it his library as early as 1932. He was a bachelor, and, when he died in 1976, the collection came in its entirety to Trinity. The library itself contained between 16,000 and 17,000 volumes when Ray inherited it in 1926, and he managed to maintain it at what librarians today would call 'steady state', that is to say he sold off less important items when he acquired new and more valuable ones, because he had run out of space for expansion in the family house. The library already occupied three communicating rooms at Dry Close, plus the large library room itself (possibly built by his father after the First World War).

The collecting policy of the library was, essentially, focused on the acquisition of illustrated books, with a particular concentration on English fine colour-plate books from the period 1780 to 1840. At the time of its acquisition by Trinity, this part of the collection alone probably represented one of the finest of its sort still in private hands. This was only one section of the collection (some 750 volumes); it also contained illuminated manuscripts, both western and eastern; some twenty-four incunabula (books printed between the invention of printing with movable type c. 1455 and 1500); many other important early printed books from the sixteenth to eighteenth centuries, including early editions of Hobbes, Locke and Adam Smith; a small number of modern first editions; a complete run of volumes containing illustrations by Arthur Rackham; some dozen or so books with their fore-edges painted; approximately 450 volumes of erotica (some of considerable rarity); a collection of several hundred books printed by small private presses throughout the first half of the twentieth century; and books relating to military history, with a particular emphasis on the British Army in the First World War. In addition to these 'special collections', there was also a general 'reference collection', including runs of learned journals, other reference works, and books on exploration and travel.

The library was bequeathed to Trinity in Ray Danson's will. He stipulated that he would like the College to retain and house certain parts of the

J. R. Danson's bookplate

collection, particularly the colour-plate books, and, if possible, to keep the erotica, although they could be placed on deposit in the Bodleian Library; other material could be sold, if the College wished, and the proceeds used for 'purposes connected with the library'. In fact, the College has chosen to retain the bulk of the special collections, although many of the private press books were subsequently sold. Whilst the manuscripts are now deposited, with the rest of the College's manuscript collection, in the Bodleian Library, the incunabula and other early printed books, the colour-plate books, the Rackhams, painted fore-edge volumes, and the erotica are all housed within the College, in the Danson Library adjacent to the Old Library.

The room which forms the Danson Library had originally been part of the College Presidents' accommodation and was, in more recent years, used as a teaching room. The initial library layout, with grilled bookcases, did not display the collection to the best advantage, so a renovation was planned to make the whole collection more accessible, with more appropriate shelving for the large folios, and additional shelving for a number of books from the Old Library which had previously been stored on the window sills.

Work on the reconfiguration started in June 2010 and was completed in 2011. The College carpenters designed and constructed new bookcases in American oak, which was then French-polished in a lighter stain than the Old Library, to create a visual contrast. As the bookcases, even without books, weigh 6.5 tonnes, the floor was strengthened with steel girders. A time-capsule, containing College memorabilia from 2011, and photographs of the carpenters, was hidden within the room.

The reconfiguration of the Danson Library had the benefit of providing further shelving for existing and future donations and bequests. The Library already housed the Chadwyck-Healey Bible collection and, in recent years notable additions have included books from the estate of Edgar Wind, the first Oxford University Professor in the History of Art; a collection of twentieth-century Faber & Faber art history books from Trinity Old Member Giles de la Mare, as well as individual donations from college members and Fellows.

The Danson Library bookshelves.

Leo I, Pont. Max., *Sermones*, ed. Johannes Andreae

(Rome: Conrad Sweynheym & Arnold Pannartz, 1470)

St Leo I, Pope from 440 until 461, is chiefly remembered as the Pope who persuaded the Huns to withdraw over the Danube in 452, and who obtained concessions from the Vandals when they took Rome three years later. These achievements exemplify the extent to which he extended and consolidated the influence of the Papacy. Some ninety-seven of his sermons survive, and it is these which are printed in this handsome incunable edition of 1470. The printers, Conrad Sweynheym and Arnold Pannartz, were the two Germans who brought the recent invention of printing with movable type from Germany into Italy, establishing themselves first in the monastery of Subiaco, before settling in Rome.

This copy is bound in a handsome, contemporary Italian blind-tooled binding, with beautiful knot-work decoration, which gives the covers an almost oriental look. The illuminated first leaf of the work shows hand-painted vine-stem decoration, also contemporary, and probably Roman. The book forms part of the Danson bequest, having been purchased by Sir Francis Danson in 1922.

William Blake, *Illustrations for the Book of Job*

(London, 1826)

William Blake, the author of *Songs of Innocence and Experience* and the 'Preface' to *Milton* (now better known as the hymn 'Jerusalem'), was also a skilled artist and a prodigious engraver. These illustrations, his last completed commission before his death in 1827, are arguably the greatest testament to his talents. Like most of Blake's works, they failed to attract commercial interest during his lifetime, but after his death they were acclaimed by notable critics including John Ruskin.

Blake was an insightful yet idiosyncratic reader of the biblical text. He imbues his illustrations with dense scriptural allusions and often highlights intriguing pieces of text from the King James Version of Job in order to set the story in a new and surprising light.

A set of illustrations was donated to the College in 1899 by a former undergraduate, Alfred Vaughan Paton. He most likely donated the prints to be studied and enjoyed by the College students. The prints remained in semi-obscurity in the Library's collection until they were rediscovered in 2012 by Trinity graduate student Jonathan Downing. Subsequent research revealed that they are part of the initial 150 print-run which Blake and Linnell commissioned, as many of the pages contain the unique watermark 'J Whatman, Turkey Mill, 1825'.

Aesop, *Fables*, trans. V. S. Vernon Jones,
intr. G. K. Chesterton, ill. Arthur Rackham
(London: Heinemann, 1912)

THE CAT AND THE COCK

This edition of Aesop's *Fables* introduced by the essayist, poet, author, and literary critic, G. K. Chesterton (1874–1936), contains twelve full-page illustrations in colour, and fifty-three drawings in black and white by the well-known illustrator, particularly of children's books, Arthur Rackham (1867–1939). Rackham studied art at evening classes at the Lambeth School of Art, whilst working in business during the day. By the time of the publication of this edition of Aesop, Rackham had already established himself as in imaginative and powerful illustrator of books: indeed, his real renown began in 1900, with the publication of the *Fairy Tales of the Brothers Grimm*. Exhibitions of his work followed, and the Christmas gift-book trade proved to be an excellent market for him.

Rackham's style is highly distinctive, and has been described as Nordic or Gothic. From his imagination came a fantasy world full of weird and rather sinister animals, birds, fairies, trees, and people. This copy of Aesop is number 1142 of a limited edition of 1450, and is autographed by the illustrator. It was bought by Ray Danson, along with a number of other limited edition books illustrated by Rackham.

Aesop, *Fables*, trans. Roger L'Estrange,
with plates and decorations by Stephen Gooden
(London: Harrap & Co., 1936)

Sir Roger L'Estrange (1616–1704), whose translation is used in this particular edition, was a well-known Restoration pamphleteer, writer, and journalist. A somewhat controversial figure, he was knighted by James II in 1685, but was viewed with suspicion after the Glorious Revolution of 1688, and was frequently imprisoned. His translation of Aesop was first published in 1692.

The illustrations are the work of Stephen Gooden (1892-1955), an engraver who worked primarily as a book illustrator and bookplate designer. He is best known for his engravings for the Nonesuch Press, a private press founded in 1922. This copy of Aesop, from the Danson bequest, is number eight of a limited edition of 525, and is autographed by Gooden.

S. Gulielmus Ebor.   Sanctus Benedictus.

The Medieval Glass

Introduction

There is uncertainty regarding the original situation and arrangement of the glass that is now preserved in the east windows of the Old Library. As it has often been suggested that this glass is the remnant of the medieval glazing of the old Chapel, it is worth examining first what is known about the decoration of the windows of that building.

Erected in 1406–08 and dedicated in 1409, the old Chapel was a structure of three bays. A window dominated each bay and there was, in addition, a window at the east end. Clearly shown in Loggan's engraving of 1675, the windows on the south side consisted of three large lights surmounted by four smaller ones, capped and flanked by small tracery panels. Perpendicular windows were well suited to housing series of figures, each standing in its own depicted niche; and this appears to have been the nature of the decorative programme, a common one in the fourteenth and fifteenth centuries. For more specific information we are dependent on the notes of John Aubrey, antiquary and Trinity member. He reported that the east window of the Chapel contained 'northerne coates' and an orate for Thomas Pope, the latter a post-medieval addition. His other comment relates to the figural work: 'the windows here were very good Gothique painting like those of New College and I think better, in every columne a figure eg St Cuthbert, St Leonard, St Oswald, I have forgott the rest. Tis pitty they should be lost'. Aubrey also explained the circumstances under which they were 'lost': 'The glass of these windows in the time of the Presbiter Government were taken down and now there is only plain glass'. Whether this phrase implies that it was removed and consigned to storage, as opposed to being destroyed, is unclear. Towards the end of the seventeenth century, on the initiative of President Bathurst, the old Chapel was demolished to make way for the present one, which was begun in 1691. Bathurst, who was energetic in rebuilding and refurbishing the fabric, also had the medieval glass of the Library removed. Consequently, if all or some of the early glass of the old Chapel had been stored, this provides a context in which it could have been joined to, and could have subsequently replaced, the surviving original Library glass in the windows of the Old Library. A descriptive account of the glass in the Library was written in 1765, and shows that little of significance has subsequently been lost; however, other than noting that one figure, two heads, and an inscription had previously been in the old vestry, the writer made no comment on the original situation of the various figures that had been replaced in the Library windows well before his time.

The construction of the Old Library post-dated that of the old Chapel by a decade, while fittings were added and one window, at least, was glazed (presumably a re-glazing). Aubrey's notes are again helpful concerning the original figural decoration of the glass. He observed that the Library 'had originally an arched roof, as appears by a view of the south end window. This as well as the rest of the windows was adorned with figures of painted glass representing the benefactors to this seminary'. His information can be supplemented by a note pasted into Anthony Wood's account of Durham College: 'In Trinity College library which did sometimes belong to Durham College there was an image of John of Beverly in the windowes with some mention of his name'.

For the subsequent fate of the windows in the Library we return to Aubrey who reports that they were 'much injured at the Reformation and by the misguided zeal of the independent soldiers during the rebellion'. According to the account of the glass drawn up in 1765, all the names and legends were destroyed at this time. The next stage in the history of the glass was, as mentioned above, its removal from the windows through the initiative of Dr Bathurst. A guide to the arrangement of some of the glass in the Library before Bathurst's time is preserved in the notes and sketches made by William Dugdale on 28 April 1646 (Bodleian Library, MS Dugdale 11, fols. 148v-149r); however, other than recording the presence of a (now lost) kneeling figure, dressed in purple, facing left, and accompanied by an orate inscription, this concentrates on the heraldry and offers no information about the figures. The next important source is the document of 1765. In that year, glass that was apparently scattered throughout various windows in the Library was reset so as to fill the five windows on the west side, and a careful description of the rearrangement was written by William Huddesford, Fellow of the College and Keeper of the Ashmolean. He noted which parts of the glass were restorations and recorded the previous locations of the figures. With the exception of the one figure and two heads from the vestry mentioned above, all the figures whose earlier position he reported were already in the Library. The account itself is scholarly, but it is sobering to note how little was known about the glass even in 1765. Huddesford introduced his account by stating that the work done in 1765 followed 'several imperfect reparations at different periods', and he admitted that the identity of many of the figures was unknown, heading his suggested identifications 'Speculations'.

In 1878, under President Wayte, the figures were moved to the windows on the east side of the Library and the (speculative) naming inscriptions were added. This is substantially the arrangement to be seen today, for, although the glass was removed again in the 1950s to repair decayed leading, all the figures in the east windows were replaced as found.

Given so confused and inadequately documented a history, it would be unwise to be dogmatic about the origin of the glass now in the Library. It is clear that the architectural niches were not designed for their present settings since they have had to be truncated to fit the Library lights, and it is probable, then, that they came from the Chapel. However, with the exception of two of the diminutive praying figures, there is no reason to presume that the figures were originally associated with the depicted niches they now inhabit. By virtue of their subject, the four evangelists and John the Baptist are more likely to have been designed for the Chapel than for the Library; but the subject of the episcopal saint was no less appropriate for the one place than for the other, and such a figure is documented in both. The surviving archbishops are not all work of the same period. There is a noticeable stylistic distinction and also a difference in size between the archbishops in lights 2 and 4 of window 3, and the other archbishops and the pope; the former are probably work of an earlier period than the latter. If it is assumed that the Chapel was given its painted glass at the time it was built, one might reasonably infer that the two earlier figures came from the Chapel, while the later ones belonged to the Library. One reconstruction of the decorative scheme of the Library windows that could incorporate the remaining saintly archbishops and also be consistent with the accounts of both Wood and Aubrey is a series of the canonised archbishops of York, accompanied by benefactors to the College such as Bishops Hatfield and Langley.

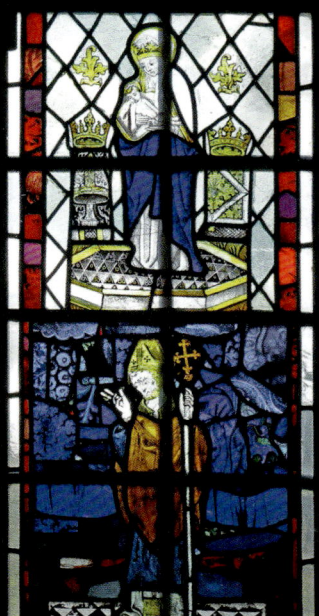

The South Window

The tracery light features three angels supporting a shield with the arms of Thomas Hatfield (inset). Dating from the second quarter of the fifteenth century, it is the only medieval glass in the Library still in its original position.

The Durham College accounts record that in 1436 a payment of 28s 8d was made for the glazing of a window in the Library, and this probably refers to the south window as a whole. If so, as the window contains approximately 18 square feet of glass, the glazier received about 1s 6d per square foot. This compares favourably with the rate of 1s per square foot that All Souls College paid John Glazier in 1441 for his work in its Chapel.

The glass in the south window today represents the repositioning of a miscellany of painted glass, returned to the College after cleaning and repairs, and installed in its present location through the generosity of the Forster family in 2003. It contains some panels, such as the coats of arms of the University of Oxford and of Richard, third Duke of York (1411–60), which had been in that window for a long time before their removal for cleaning. However, the window now also includes some glass, such as the full-length archbishop, the small full-length bishop and the haloed queen, which had presumably been placed in the Old Library probably in the later part of the seventeenth century by President Bathurst, then removed during the 1878 restoration and placed in the east-facing window of the old Senior Common Room on the first floor overlooking the Durham Quad. It was, therefore, logical to have them reinstated in the Old Library. The full-length archbishop with a praying monk at his feet is clearly from the same series as the ecclesiastics in east window 3, as too is the head of the otherwise lost archbishop that forms the centrepiece of the light above.

The small plaque commemorates the poet Thomas Warton (1728–1790), sometime Fellow of the College. It was given in 1790 by his sister, Jane Warton (1724–1809).

There is also a small panel of miscellaneous glass in one of the windows on the staircase up to the Old Library, consisting of fragments for which space could not be found in the south window; this was placed there in 2005–06.

The East Windows

The east wall has four windows, each with four lights. All sixteen lights contain a figure set within an architectural niche. The truncation of the depicted architecture imposed by the shape and size of the lights (especially noticeable in the lower lights of windows 3 and 4, numbered from the north end of the Library), the differing sizes of the figures, and the use of fragments of displaced glass to make them fit the niches (most obtrusive in window 3) serve as vivid reminders of the history of damage, displacement and restoration behind the particular ensemble of glass that has survived.

The use of architectural niches to provide a setting for individual is found in painted glass from the end of the thirteenth century. During the fourteenth and fifteenth centuries the architectural forms used grew in complexity, and from the second half of the fourteenth century designers were increasingly concerned to impart to their structures an illusion of recession. Two contemporaneous types of niche can be seen in the east windows. The lower lights of windows 1 and 2 have a robust, relatively squat structure, with recessive open arches in the side walls and a roof angled so as to give an illusion of forward projection. Pinnacles (now truncated) extend above the body of the structure. The niche type found in varying states of preservation in the other lights follows a taller design with a more elaborate superstructure of pinnacles (again truncated) and with solid rather than open-arched sides. The generous use of crocketed pinnacles is a common feature in fifteenth-century glass, and the choice of white glass for the architecture, with some of the structural details being outlined in yellow stain, was also customary at this date. Comparison may be made with the architectural niches depicted in the windows of the antechapel of All Souls. There figures stand on pedestals with a patterned surface that contributes to the illusion of a recessional setting. Fragments of similar patterned surfaces can be seen beneath a number of the Old Library figures, and nearly complete tiled pedestals are still attached to the feet of figures 2 and 4 in window 3.

Although all conceived in a semi-naturalistic manner, entirely consonant with a date in the first half of the fifteenth century, the figures in the Old Library display a variety of styles. There is a noticeable contrast between figures 2 and 4 in window 3 (Thomas Becket and 'Dunstan'), and the other archbishops and the pope. The former are slender and graceful with a residual S-curve pose; the latter are stocky and solid. John the Baptist and the female saint in light 1 of window 1 are also less bulky figures, but they do not share the distinctive curved posture of Thomas and 'Dunstan'; the curve does, however, reappear in the figure of John the Evangelist. If the stocky ecclesiastics may be compared with John Glazier's mid fifteenth-century saints in the antechapel of All Souls College, the figures of Thomas and 'Dunstan' recall Thomas Glazier's work at New College about half a century earlier, while John the Baptist and perhaps also John the Evangelist can be compared with the slightly later figures of Thomas Glazier's workshop in Merton College.

By the fifteenth century, larger pieces of glass were used to construct painted windows. All the figures in the Library have their head and halo rendered on one piece of glass. This is a point of contrast with the work at Merton, New College and All Souls, where heads and halos are often spread across several pieces. The faces of the figures in the Library have all been designed to suggest a measure of individual characterisation, but by far the finest head is that of John the Baptist. A restricted palette was used for the figures, most of whom are clothed in a white mantle over a single-coloured robe; but then extensive use was made of yellow stain (created by painting with silver oxide on white glass before it was fired) for adding details and decorative patterns to the white areas. Halos, hair and garments were also added in this way. The general scheme of a figure dressed in two robes, one white, one coloured, and set against a patterned red or blue surround was common for figural windows in the fifteenth century. Another feature of such windows was the naming inscription that accompanied each figure. The inscriptions in the Library windows, it will be recalled, date from the nineteenth century and in many cases have no particular authority. The loss of the original texts and the lack of a written account of them is greatly to be regretted since it leaves the identity of most of the figures uncertain. The only figures that can clearly be identified on iconographic grounds are John the Baptist, Thomas of Canterbury and the four evangelists; the original identity of the others is a matter of speculation.

Sanctus Placidus

Sancta Frideswida

East Window 1

1. Top left

Crowned, haloed, female saint, turned to the right, holding in her right hand a staff which terminates in a small cross, holding in her left a book; very restored. To the left a small, blue-robed, tonsured figure, kneeling in prayer. Above him a scroll inscribed 'Deus / .??ie ·tuo ·sa / me ·fac'. Figure, scroll and hatched background do not belong to the architecture of the niche.

Shield: arms of Grey impaling Mowbray.

This crowned female saint is probably the figure formerly believed to represent Queen Philippa – a theory vitiated by the halo. A more plausible identification for a saintly queen would be Margaret of Scotland (d. 1093), who was a benefactress of Durham Cathedral, celebrated for her learning as well as her piety. The small figure corresponds with that described by Huddesford as 'a smaller figure praying, and near him a scroll with these words, "Deus in nomine tuo salvum me fac" ("God, in your name, save me"). In 1765 he was placed in the fifth window on the west side by the feet of 'a woman in a hood and crosier'. Huddesford records that he was 'formerly in the old vestry'. The shield is that of Thomas Grey (d. 1401) and his wife Jane Mowbray. They were presumably benefactors of Durham College.

2. Top right

'Sanctus Placidus'. Haloed Benedictine abbot, turned to the left, holding a crozier around which is a drape. The figure is entirely restoration apart from the panel of the head. To the left a small, blue robed, tonsured, praying figure. His head is painted on one of the panels of architecture. The architecture beneath him is displaced.

None of the written sources specifies a figure of Placidus. This nineteenth-century inscription was presumably felt to represent a reasonable choice of identity because Placidus was a popular saint in Benedictine establishments and was regarded as the patron of novices. 'Placidus' may be the figure placed in the fifth window on the west side in 1765, which Huddesford described as 'a figure of a Benedictine monk – at his feet a smaller one praying [...] The body of the figure is new. It was formerly in the fourth window'. The identity of the figure was then uncertain and the name Cuthbert had been chosen for it.

3. Bottom left

'Sancta Frideswida'. Benedictine nun with veil, crozier and book, turned to the right. All restoration except the panel of the head and the central panel with hands and book. The restored robe is blue, but on the central panel a brown garment can be seen. The veil is also brown.

The identification of a female figure in the Library as St Frideswide was first conjecturally made in 1765 'she being a local saint and patroness of Oxford'. The figure so named was then in the fifth window on the west side. She was described by Huddesford as 'a woman in a hood and crosier [...] the lower part from the neck is painted', which would seem to be this figure. More likely identifications are SS. Hilda (d. 680) or Æbbe (d. 683). The former, who was related to the royal families of both Northumbria and East Anglia, became Abbess of Hartlepool, then Whitby; her zeal for education may have recommended her as a subject for a window in Durham's Oxford college. The latter, the daughter of King Æthelfrith of Northumbria, became Abbess of Coldingham; as Coldingham was a cell of Durham, as Durham itself possessed relics of Æbbe, and as there was also a church in Oxford dedicated to her, she would have been a strong candidate for commemoration in a window.

4. Bottom right

Canonised king, turned to the left, holding orb and sceptre. He wears a blue cloak over a white robe with a yellow stain pattern and fringe. To the left a small kneeling monk in a blue robe. His head and white hood are painted on one of the panels of architecture. In the present arrangement, his legs have nothing on which to kneel.

Shield: Angerville.

A figure with crown, globe and sceptre, with a monk praying at his feet, below the arms of Richard Angerville, was regarded in 1765 as Edward III; it was recorded to have come from window 2 on the east side. Given Bishop Hatfield's association with Edward III and his stipulation that prayers should be said for him at Durham College, the inclusion of the king among the figures depicted in the College windows would seem reasonable. However, the halo of this king (opposite) precludes the possibility that he was meant to represent Edward. A more credible suggestion would be Oswald, a saint particularly venerated at Durham. Oswald, King of Northumbria, was killed in 642 by the Mercian ruler Penda, thereby establishing a claim to martyrdom. Penda had Oswald's body dismembered and hung on stakes, but the pieces were recovered and venerated in different places. His head came to Lindisfarne and was placed in St Cuthbert's coffin, moving with the Lindisfarne community first to Chester-le-Street and then to Durham in 995. Oswald was one of the northern saints whom Aubrey remembered having seen in the windows of the College Chapel. The possibility that this was the figure in question should not be discounted; however stylistically he is akin to the archbishops and the pope for whom an origin in the Library has here been suggested.

The shield (opposite) is possibly that of Richard de Bury (1281–1345), son of Richard Angerville. De Bury studied at Oxford and then became a monk at Durham; he was Edward III's tutor and, as a result of the king's favour, subsequently enjoyed both civil and ecclesiastical preferment, being made Bishop of Durham in 1333. It is appropriate that his arms should be preserved in the Library since his love of books and libraries is reflected in his work, *Philobiblon*, concerning the acquisition and organisation of books

S Gulielmus Ebor

Sanctus Benedictus

S Swithin

S Johannes Bpta

East Window 2

1. Top left

'S Wulielmus Ebor'. Haloed archbishop, facing right, wearing mitre, chasuble and pallium, holding a cross staff in his left hand.

Shield: Percy quartering Lucy.

There is no reason to think that this particular figure was originally William of York; however, it is fairly likely that he was included in the series of archbishop saints. William Fitzherbert was appointed Archbishop of York in 1141 but failed to obtain the pallium (a vestment conferred by a pope on an archbishop) from four successive popes, the last of whom, Eugenius III, deposed him in 1148. Pope Anastasius IV reappointed him to the see in 1153, but he died, perhaps as a result of poison, in 1154. He was canonised in 1227. Although his life story seems uninspiring and representations of him are rare outside York, his cult was vigorously promoted there, so it is not improbable that he was one of the northern saints commemorated at Durham College. Furthermore, Thomas Langley was bishop of Durham from 1406 to 1437 – during the period when both the Chapel and the Library were constructed – and had been Dean of York between 1401 and 1406. He was a notable benefactor to Durham College; Wood records that his arms appeared both in the Library and in a chamber underneath it. The erection in 1421 in York Minster of a great window showing sixty-two scenes of the life, death, miracles and translation of William of York may have provided a further stimulus for including the saint in the glass at Durham College.

The shield commemorates the marriage, in 1381, of Henry Percy, first Earl of Northumberland, and Maud, heiress of the Lucy family. The Lucy estates passed to the Percy family on condition that they quartered the Lucy arms with their own. These arms are presumably those of a child or descendant of Henry Percy, possibly Henry, second Earl of Northumberland.

2. Top right

Haloed monk, facing left, holding a book in his right hand. Modern inscription Ben[e]dictus. To the left, small, kneeling, secular figure, wearing a white robe with a brown fur collar. Below him, scroll inscribed Johannes Tokot.

Shield (modern): Percy.

The use of a deep blue to represent a black robe, seen on the large saint here and on some of the small praying figures, was common, given the difficulty and impracticality of engineering black in painted glass. It is possible that the figure was intended for St Benedict – a Benedictine foundation is highly likely to have included the founder of their order amongst the saints they had depicted. Benedict's most common iconographic attributes were a broken cup, a raven, a book and a rod. The image of St Benedict recorded to have featured in the glass of Durham Cathedral itself showed him wearing a black (blue) habit and holding a crozier. An alternative identity worth considering is the Venerable Bede (d. 735), whom the iconography would equally suit. His relics were at Durham, and his enduring scholarly reputation would have made him a particularly appropriate subject for a window in its Oxford College.

As the head of the small, kneeling figure is painted on one of the panels of architecture, it clearly belongs to it. However, the panel with the inscription is evidently misplaced. It has not proved possible to trace an individual by the name of John Tokot. The presence of a diminutive donor figure or a naming inscription is a common feature of painted glass from the thirteenth century onwards, and examples appear prominently in the chapel of Merton College and the antechapel of New College. Whereas in these cases the named individuals (Henry de Mamesfeld and William of Wykeham respectively) were the patrons of the new windows, at Durham College the cost of the glazing presumably came from a corporate purse (it was certainly thus for the Library window glazed in 1436). It is possible that the diminutive figures represented not donors of specific windows but rather members of Durham College shown perpetually in the act of praying to and for the saints and benefactors of their foundation, as Bishop Hatfield's statutes had enjoined, while at the same time requesting prayers and blessings for themselves. The inclusion of both secular and monastic praying figures is consonant with Hatfield's provision for the presence of eight secular students at the College.

3. *Bottom left*

'S Swithun'. Haloed bishop, turned to the right, blessing with his right hand, holding in his left a crozier, around the staff of which is a band of material. He appears truncated in comparison with the other ecclesiastics and has probably

lost a panel from his waist area. To the right a small untonsured figure, kneeling in prayer, wearing a white robe with a lavish brown fur hood.

The identity of this bishop is uncertain. There is no reason to think that Swithun, associated with Winchester, would have been commemorated at Durham College. More likely candidates are Aidan (d. 651), first Bishop and abbot of Lindisfarne, or Cuthbert, Bishop of Lindisfarne 685–87, who was especially venerated, and his cult was fostered, by the Durham community.

Whatever the original identity of this figure, Cuthbert was one of the saints specified by Aubrey as depicted in the glass of the Chapel. Production of an image of Cuthbert at Durham College came at a time when there was a revival of interest in creating elaborate cycles of scenes from his life. Around 1420, windows decorated with a cycle of his life were placed in the cloister of Durham Cathedral, with another one at the south end of the Chapel of the Nine Altars; a decade later a Cuthbert window was commissioned for York Minster. These were all the gift of Thomas Langley, who was also a benefactor to Durham College.

4. Bottom right

John the Baptist, depicted as a standing figure, turned to the left, with flowing hair and beard, wearing a complete, yellow camel skin under his mantle, its hooves and skull at his feet. The Agnus Dei (Lamb of God) appears on the book which John holds in draped hands.

The figure (illustrated on the back cover) is the finest in the Library, and it has been compared with the glass at Merton College ascribed to the workshop of Thomas Glazier. This type of John the Baptist is characteristic of the fifteenth century. The lamb bears apocalyptic connotations, but is carried by John in reference to the fact that, when Jesus came to him for baptism, he exclaimed, 'Behold the Lamb of God which takes away the sin of the world' (John 1.29). The fact that the lamb is borne on an open book alludes to the fulfilment of Old Testament prophecies about the Lamb (e.g. Isaiah 53.7, Jeremiah 11.1) and evokes the book with seven seals that only the Lamb was worthy to open (Revelation 5).

Sanctus Gregorius

Sanctus Thomas Cant

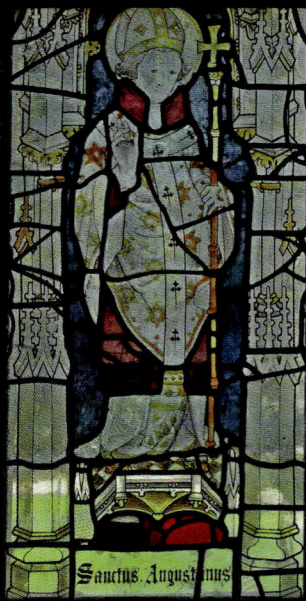

Sanctus Augustinus

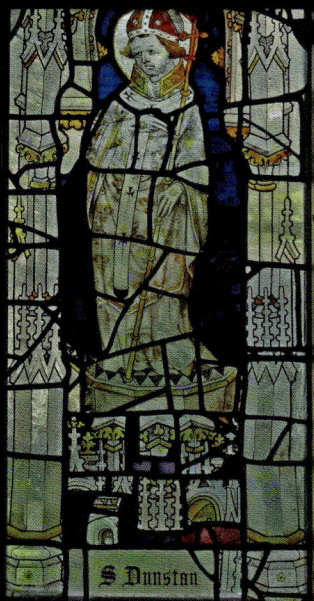

S Dunstan

East Window 3

1. Top left

'Sanctus Gregorius'. Haloed pope, turned to the right, wearing a single-peaked mitre surrounded by a crown, blessing with his right hand, holding a double crossed staff in his left. Little restored.

Shield: Wessington (Washington).

It is difficult to think of a better choice than Gregory the Great (d. 604) for the identity of the pope represented here. We know that Gregory was represented elsewhere in the College, for he was one of the two figures that adorned the glass of Aubrey's room.

The arms are those of John Washington. Washington (d. 1451), one of the Durham monks sent to Oxford for his education, became Bursar of Durham College in 1398, and Prior at Durham in 1422.

2. Top right

'Sanctus Thomas Cants'. Haloed archbishop, wearing mitre and pallium, turned to the left, blessing with right hand, holding a single crossed staff in his left. The broken-off tip of a sword protrudes from his forehead just below his mitre.

Shield (modern): Washington.

3. Bottom left

'Sanctus Augustinus'. Haloed archbishop wearing mitre and pallium, turned to the right, blessing with right hand, holding a single crossed staff in his left. Little restored.

4. Bottom right

'S Dunstan'. Haloed archbishop, turned to the left, wearing mitre and pallium, his right hand across his breast, his left holding a single crossed staff.

There are clear distinctions in size and style between the figures in the right hand lights of this window and those on the left. Figures 1 and 3 in window 2 and the archbishop now in the bottom left of the south window belong to the same series as the archbishops on the left.

The only figure in window 3 clearly identified iconographically is number two. The tip of a sword projecting from this archbishop's forehead shows him to be Thomas Becket. When the saint was depicted with the sword in his skull, he was generally shown bare headed; the Old Library figure is uncommon in having a head that features both a sword tip and a mitre.

Well-preserved depictions of Becket are comparatively rare in English medieval art for, in addition to the general ravages of time, they were specially targeted for destruction by Henry VIII. Discreet scratches on the forehead of the figure may have been effected as a response to the royal injunction of 1538 that demanded the destruction of images of the saint – showing a politic obedience to the letter of the law, while disobeying its spirit.

It is unsurprising that Becket, who was widely venerated, appears among the saints depicted in the Durham College glass, but his presence establishes that it was not only saints of a northern connection who were shown. It is not impossible that the other two Canterbury archbishop-saints, Ælphege and Dunstan, were also included. It seems more likely, however, that the archiepiscopal figures were predominantly saintly incumbents of the see of York. Wood, it will be recalled, noted that John of Beverley (Bishop of York from 705 to 717) appeared in the Library, and the likelihood that William of York appeared in the Durham College glass was noted above in relation to window 2. The other bishops of York who were recognised as saints, and so could be candidates for inclusion, were Paulinus, Chad, Wilfrid, Bosa, Wilfrid II and Egbert. Although Egbert was the first holder of the see to be recognised as an archbishop and so, strictly speaking, only he and William were entitled to be shown wearing a pallium, such niceties of historical accuracy are unlikely to have concerned the patrons and designers of windows in the fifteenth century.

East Window 4

1. Top left

'Sanctus Marcus'. Bearded figure, turned to the right, dressed in a white mantle over a purple robe. He holds a book (his gospel) in his draped left hand and points to it with his (barely visible) right hand. His symbol, a haloed lion without wings, protrudes from behind his legs.

As it is unlikely that one symbol lacked wings when the others had them, a piece of glass which included an upraised wing and originally fitted above the lion's halo, has probably been lost.

2. Top right

'Sanctus Mattheus'. Frontal figure with wings and luxuriant beard, wearing a white mantle over a blue robe. He holds a book in his left hand and gestures towards it with his right.

The wings and the absence of a separate symbol figure indicate that in this case the evangelist and his symbol, the angel, have been conflated.

3. Bottom left

'Sanctus Johannes'. A young beardless figure, facing right, holding a palm in his right hand and clutching a book in his draped left hand. He wears a purple robe and a white mantle. His symbol, the eagle, appears behind his legs.

John (right) was customarily depicted as a younger man than the other evangelists. The palm that he holds here may allude to his suffering (though not martyrdom) under the Emperor Domitian and/or to an element in the story of the assumption of Mary: a palm was said to have been brought to the Virgin by the angel who announced her impending death, and she gave it to John to carry before her bier.

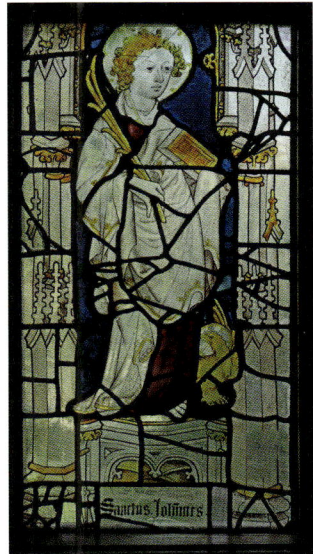

Sanctus Marcus

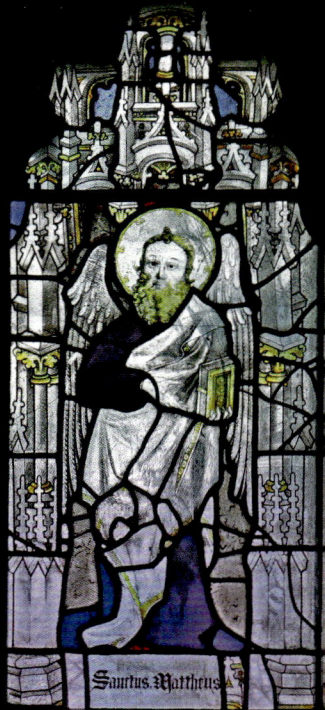

Sanctus Mattheus

Sanctus Johnnes

Sanctus Lukas

4. Bottom right

'Sanctus Lukas'. Bearded figure turned to the left, holding a book in his draped right hand. He wears a blue robe under his white mantle. A winged ox appears behind his legs. Very restored.

Huddesford recorded 'This figure is composed of various pieces, nothing of the original remaining except the calf [...] The head belonged to another figure and was taken out of a window in an old room next to the chapel, formerly the vestry'. Aubrey noted, more specifically, that the figure to whom the head had belonged was John the Baptist. The present head is not the one to which Huddesford and Aubrey referred; rather it appears to be a modern restoration reproducing in reverse the head of St Matthew (both shown below). Whether the head that they saw is that which belongs to the surviving figure of John the Baptist (having then been restored to him in the nineteenth century) is uncertain, but unlikely.

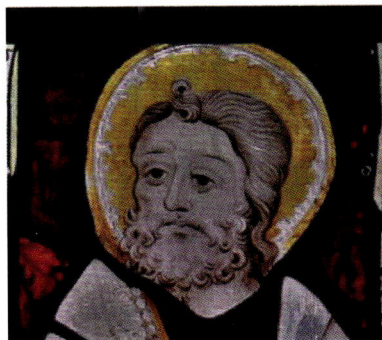

The West Windows (Later Glass)

The west windows (see illustration on p. 14) contain small but striking images of ten virtues and six saints, all dating from the seventeenth century. They were moved to the Old Library from the Hall, in 1878.

The 'virtues', below, are from west window 2.

The Library Furniture

Although none of the original Old Library furnishings remain in situ, the Library houses some fine antique furniture, notably from the Cumberbatch bequest (see p. 64). The present arrangement dates from the 2011 renovation of the Danson Library, and includes some particularly interesting additions associated with distinguished former members of the College.

Also in the Library are four busts; three are plaster and one is coloured bronze. These depict: Ralph Bathurst (1620–1704), College President from 1664 to 1704; Christopher Wren (1632–1723), the original architect of the Garden Quadrangle and adviser on the design of Trinity's celebrated Chapel; Thomas Lee (1761–1824), College President 1808–24; and William Alexander Greenhill (1814–94), Trinity graduate, physician and sanitary reformer. The busts were originally displayed on wooden plinths on the west side of the Library, and the window sills still bear the scars from their removal.

Bust of President Ralph Bathurst.

Thomas Warton's Chair

Thomas Warton (1728–1790), the poet, biographer, and historian, came to Trinity as an undergraduate in 1744, and remained at the College for the rest of his life, having been elected Fellow in 1752. While he was a serious scholar, Warton had another side, as humourist and satirist. This reached its apotheosis when he contributed to and edited (anonymously) *The Oxford Sausage, or, Select Poetical Pieces written by the most celebrated Wits of the University of Oxford* (London: J. Fletcher and Co., 1764).

Sometime in the early 1750s, Warton met Samuel Johnson and they developed a lifelong friendship. Johnson obtained permission, through Warton, to use the Old Library for his studies. Boswell later wrote in his *Life of Johnson*: 'Of this library, which is

Thomas Warton
by Sir Joshua Reynolds.

an old Gothic room, he was very fond. On my observing to him, that some of the modern libraries of the university were more commodious and pleasant for study [...] he replied "Sir, if a man has a mind to prance then he must study at Christ Church and All Souls"'. (James Boswell, *Life of Samuel Johnson, LL. D.*, Vol. 2 Oxford: Talboys and Wheeler, 1826, p. 56.)

In 1769, Johnson presented to the College, as a mark of his affection, a fine copy of Virgil's *Works*.

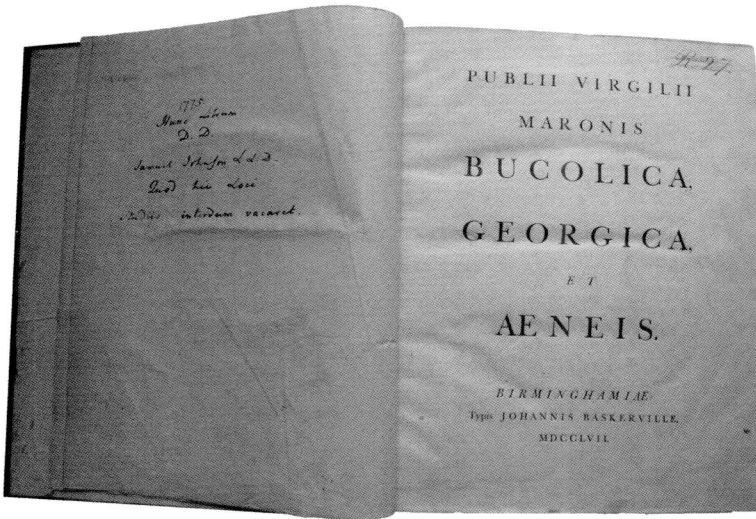

Virgil Opera *(Birmingham: John Baskerville, 1757).*

Already Professor of Poetry at Oxford from 1757–67, Thomas Warton became poet laureate upon the death of William Whitehead in 1785. Warton's chair is now displayed in the Old Library. Apparently designed and made for him, it is a unique take on the eighteenth century Windsor spindle-backed design, incorporating cabriole legs and splayed arms. On 20 May 1790, Warton suffered a paralytic stroke whilst sitting in this chair. He died the following day and was buried in the Trinity ante-chapel, where the commemorative flagstone is still visible.

Robert Raper's Chair

Robert William Raper (1842–1915) arrived at the University as a Balliol undergraduate in 1861, but in his first term, he moved to Trinity after being elected a scholar. He obtained the university prizes for Greek and Latin verse in 1862, followed by a first-class degree in 1865. In 1871, he was elected to a Fellowship at Trinity and subsequently took a leading part in the administration of the College, becoming Senior Bursar and Vice President. He would probably have been elected President in 1878 if laymen had been eligible; he subsequently declined the Presidency on three occasions.

Raper also acquired extensive influence in the wider University as a Curator of the Parks from 1885, and of the Botanic Garden from 1887 to 1899. He is probably best remembered as the founder of the Appointments Committee (now the Careers Service) in 1892. He died at College in July 1915, and is commemorated in a memorial window in the Hall, which was installed in 1920.

The chair pictured above, made for Raper and now kept in the Old Library, was designed with a rattan-cane weave seat and with angled arms to facilitate easy reading of broadsheet newspapers. It bears the inscription *Hac sella utibatur et in camera et in horto* (this chair was used both indoors and in the garden).

Metamorphic Library Chairs

Furniture that opens out into library steps was, as Clive Taylor documents (see 'Further Reading'), initially manufactured for private libraries in Europe in the mid-eighteenth century, and first patented by Robert Campbell in 1774. By the end of the eighteenth century, designers were incorporating features such as sabre-shaped legs, concave top-rails and voluted open arms into their metamorphic chairs. Furniture designers simplified and standardised the form to create an English neo-classical style chair. Metamorphic chairs became more widely popular in the Regency period, an age characterised by a fascination with mechanical curiosities.

Trinity has three metamorphic chairs dating from the early nineteenth century. The finest, a mahogany chair with a caned seat (pictured right, above) has been tentatively attributed to Morgan and Saunders, and dated to *c.* 1810–15. It has been repaired over the years and underwent serious renovation in 2009. Two regional metamorphic chairs are also on display. The first has straight reeded arms, sabre-shaped legs and a plain front seat-rail. The second, which is of better quality, is of a more traditional design, complete with voluted arms and an over-scrolled top-rail (pictured left, above). The manufacturer of these chairs is not known, but the proportions are less precise and the construction inferior to the Morgan and Saunders chair.

Caquetoire Chair

The 'caquetoire' or 'caqueteuse' style of armchair emerged during the European Renaissance and was initially popular in France. The name is derived from *caqueter* (to chat). They are often called conversation chairs as they were designed for ladies to sit together and converse. The back of the chair is characteristically high and narrow, whilst the seat is narrow at the back but splayed out in a triangle shape, to accommodate ladies' voluminous skirts.

The Trinity chair is Scottish and may date from the seventeenth century, though it has been much repaired. It came to Trinity as part of the bequest of Hugh Charles Cumberbatch in 1957. Cumberbatch, who matriculated at Trinity in 1904, left his entire estate to the College. He had inherited a notable collection of furniture and silver from his uncle, Harold Charles Moffat, himself a Trinity man. Moffat was a designer and craftsman, as well as an authority on early English oak, walnut, and English marqueterie from the end of the seventeenth century.

Further Reading

Blackiston, H. E. D., 'Some Durham College Rolls', in *Collectanea* 3, ed. M. Burrows (Oxford: Oxford Historical Society, 1896).

——, *Trinity College* (London, 1898).

Carley, James, 'John Leland and the Foundations of the Royal Library: the Westminster Inventory of 1542', *Bulletin of the Society for Renaissance Studies* 7: 1 (1989), 13-22.

Catto, J. L., 'Durham College at Oxford, 1286–1542', in *Durham Cathedral: History, Fabric and Culture*, ed. David Brown (New Haven/London: Yale U.P., 2015), pp. 458–67.

Coates, Alan, 'The Library of Durham College, Oxford', *Library History* 8 (1990), 125–31.

——, 'The Old Library, Trinity College, Oxford', *Bodleian Library Record* 13: 6 (1991), 466–78.

——, 'Benedictine Monks and their Books in Oxford', in *Benedictines in Oxford*, ed. H. Wansbrough & A. Marett-Crosby (London: Darton, Longman and Todd, 1997), pp. 79–94.

——, 'The History of Trinity's Undergraduate Libraries', *Trinity College Report* ([2000 for] 1999), 54–58.

Dobson, R. B., *Durham Priory, 1400–1450* (London: Cambridge U.P., 1973).

——, 'The Black Monks of Durham and Canterbury Colleges: Comparisons and Contrasts', in *Benedictines in Oxford*, ed. H. Wansbrough & A. Marett-Crosby (London: Darton, Longman and Todd, 1997), pp. 61–78.

——, 'The Religious Orders 1370–1500', in *Late Medieval Oxford*, ed J. I. Catto & Ralph Evans, *The History of the University of Oxford*, vol. II (Oxford: Clarendon Press, 1992), 539–79.

Doyle, A. I., *The Printed Books of the Last Monks of Durham* (Durham: Dean and Chapter of Durham, 1988).

Gameson, Richard, 'The Medieval Library', in *The Cambridge History of Libraries in Britain and Ireland,* vol. I, ed. E. Leedham-Green and T. Webber, (Cambridge: Cambridge U.P., 2006), pp. 3-50.

——, *Manuscript Treasures of Durham Cathedral* (London: Third Millennium Publishing, 2010).

Gameson, Richard & Alan Coates, *The Old Library, Trinity College, Oxford* (Oxford: Trinity College, 1988).

Hopkins, Clare, *Trinity: 450 Years of an Oxford College Community* (Oxford: Oxford U.P., 2005).

Maclagan, Michael, *Trinity College* (Oxford: Oxford U.P., revised ed., 1963).

Pantin, W. A., 'Catalogue of the Books of Durham College, Oxford, ca 1390–1400', in *Formularies which bear on the History of Oxford, ca 1204–1420*, ed. H. E. Salter et al., *Oxford Historical Society*, new series 4: 1 (1942).

Parkes, M. B., 'The Provision of Books', in *Late Medieval Oxford*, ed. J. I. Catto & Ralph Evans, *The History of the University of Oxford*, vol. II (Oxford: Clarendon Press, 1992), pp. 407–83.

Piper, A. J., 'The Libraries of the Monks of Durham', in *Medieval Scribes, Manuscripts & Libraries: Essays Presented to N. R. Ker*, ed. M.B. Parkes & Andrew G. Watson (London: Scolar Press, 1978), pp. 213–49.

Poole, Rachael, *Catalogue of Portraits in the Possession of the University, Colleges, City and County of Oxford*, vol. III (Oxford: Clarendon Press, 1926).

Royal Commission on Historical Monuments (Crawford, David Lindsay, Earl of), *An Inventory of the Historical Monuments in the City of Oxford* (London: Her Majesty's Stationery Office, 1939).

Taylor, C., *The Regency Period Metamorphic Library Chair*, MA Dissertation, University of Central Lancashire, 2009.